C000153943

Oil Spills in U.S. Coastal Waters: Background and Governance

Jonathan L. Ramseur
Specialist in Environmental Policy

September 2, 2010

Congressional Research Service

7-5700

www.crs.gov

RL33705

CRS Report for Congress —————————————————————

Prepared for Members and Committees of Congress

Summary

The impacts of an oil spill depend on the size of the spill, the rate of the spill, the type of oil spilled, and the location of the spill. Depending on timing and location, even a relatively minor spill can cause significant harm to individual organisms and entire populations. Oil spills can cause impacts over a range of time scales, from days to years, or even decades for certain spills.

On April 20, 2010, an explosion occurred at the *Deepwater Horizon* drilling platform in the Gulf of Mexico, resulting in 11 fatalities. The incident led to a significant release of oil: according to the federal government's estimate, the well released approximately 206 million gallons of oil before it was contained on July 15. The 2010 Gulf oil spill has generated considerable interest in oil spill governance issues.

This report provides background information regarding oil spills in U.S. coastal waters and identifies the legal authorities governing oil spill prevention, response, and cleanup. Based on data between 1973 and 2007, the annual number and volume of oil spills have shown declines—in some cases, dramatic declines. The 1989 *Exxon Valdez* spill in Alaskan waters played a large role in stimulating actions that contributed to this trend, particularly the decrease in the annual spill volumes.

The *Exxon Valdez* spill highlighted the need for stronger legislation, inflamed public sentiment, and spurred Congress to enact comprehensive oil spill legislation, resulting in the Oil Pollution Act of 1990 (P.L. 101-380). This law expanded and clarified the authority of the federal government and created new oil spill prevention and preparedness requirements. Moreover, the 1990 legislation strengthened existing liability provisions, providing a greater deterrent against spills.

The governing framework for oil spills in the United States remains a combination of federal, state, and international authorities. Within this framework, several federal agencies have the authority to implement oil spill regulations. Agency responsibilities can be divided into two categories: (1) oil spill response and cleanup and (2) oil spill prevention/preparedness.

Oil spill response authority is determined by the location of the spill: the U.S. Coast Guard has response authority in the U.S. coastal zone, and the Environmental Protection Agency covers the inland zone. Jurisdiction over oil spill prevention and preparedness duties is determined by the potential sources (e.g., vessels, facilities, pipelines) of oil spills.

Contents

Figures

Tables

Contacts

Introduction

Oil is a dominant source of energy in the United States, supplying the nation with approximately 40% of its energy needs. Its use is widespread, providing fuel for the transportation, industrial, and residential sectors. Vast quantities of oil continuously enter the country via vessel or pipeline and are then transported to destinations throughout the country. With such widespread use and nonstop movement, it is inevitable that some number of spills will occur.

Deepwater Horizon Oil Spill in the Gulf of Mexico

On April 20, 2010, an explosion occurred at the *Deepwater Horizon* drilling platform in the Gulf of Mexico, resulting in 11 fatalities. The incident disabled the facility and led to a full evacuation before the platform sank into the Gulf on April 22. A significant release of oil at the sea floor was soon discovered. Federal agency responders include (among others) the U.S. Coast Guard, the National Oceanic and Atmospheric Administration (NOAA), and the Environmental Protection Agency (EPA). Although authorities assert no oil has escaped from the well since July 15, some degree of response activities will continue for some time. According to the National Incident Command's Flow Rate Technical Group estimate of August 2, 2010, the well released approximately 206 million gallons of oil (4.9 million barrels) before it was contained.

For more information specific to this incident, see CRS Report R41262, *Deepwater Horizon Oil Spill: Selected Issues for Congress*, coordinated by Curry L. Hagerty and Jonathan L. Ramseur.

In addition, the following websites provide up-to-date information:

Unified Command (federal agencies and responsible parties) website, at http://www.deepwaterhorizonresponse.com/

Federal government's website for the Deepwater BP oil spill response and recovery, at http://www.restorethegulf.gov/

EPA website, at http://www.epa.gov/bpspill/

NOAA website, at http://www.noaa.gov/

Over the past few decades, several major U.S. oil spills have had lasting repercussions that transcended the local environmental and economic effects. The April 2010 oil spill in the Gulf of Mexico (see text box) has intensified interest in many oil spill-related issues.[1] Prior to the 2010 Gulf spill, the most notable example was the 1989 *Exxon Valdez* spill, which released approximately 11 million gallons (260,000 barrels) of crude oil into Prince William Sound, Alaska. The *Exxon Valdez* spill[2] produced extensive consequences beyond Alaska. According to the National Academies of Science, the *Exxon Valdez* disaster caused "fundamental changes in the way the U.S. public thought about oil, the oil industry, and the transport of petroleum products by tankers ... 'big oil' was suddenly seen as a necessary evil, something to be feared and mistrusted."[3]

This report provides background information regarding oil spills[4] in U.S. coastal waters[5] and identifies the legal authorities governing oil spill prevention, response, and cleanup.[6] The first

---

[1] See CRS Report R41262, *Deepwater Horizon Oil Spill: Selected Issues for Congress*, coordinated by Curry L. Hagerty and Jonathan L. Ramseur.

[2] Note that the *Exxon Valdez* spill ranks only 35th for spill volume on the list of international tanker spills since 1967. See International Tanker Owners Pollution Federation Limited, Historical Data, at http://www.itopf.com/stats.html.

[3] See National Research Council (NRC), *Oil in the Sea III: Inputs, Fates, and Effects*, National Academies of Science (hereinafter "NRC report"), February 2003, p. 11.

[4] In this report, "oil" refers to crude oil and petroleum products, including gasoline and other fuels, unless stated otherwise.

section highlights background issues, including oil spill statistics and potential environmental impacts. The second section discusses the legal and regulatory framework that governs oil spill prevention and response.

Background

Oil Inputs

Oil enters coastal waters of the United States from a wide variety of sources. These sources vary considerably. Some sources, such as discharges from recreational vessels, emit relatively minor amounts per individual release but have numerous annual releases, which, in aggregate, contribute a significant annual volume. Other sources, such as spills from oil tankers, release oil on a less frequent basis but have the potential to release a significant volume in one incident. These variances in frequency and volume of oil releases create different environmental impacts as well as different challenges for responders and policymakers.

All Sources

A 2003 National Research Council report groups oil releases into four categories: natural seeps, oil consumption, oil transportation, and oil extraction/production.[7] As illustrated in **Figure 1**, the majority of oil in U.S. waters comes from natural seeps—geologic openings on the ocean floor. Well-known natural seeps are found in the Gulf of Mexico and off the coast of southern California, regions with extensive oil exploration and production. Although the seeps release large volumes of oil each year,[8] the surrounding ecosystem can adapt, and even thrive, because the rate of release is relatively slow.[9]

The vast majority of oil introduced to the environment through human behavior falls into the consumption category. This category is broad in scope and includes land-based sources,[10] operational discharges from commercial vessels[11] and recreational craft,[12] and atmospheric deposition of petroleum hydrocarbons.[13] The quantitative value and the environmental fate of

---

(...continued)

[5] For the purposes of this report, "U.S. coastal waters" is defined broadly to encompass all waters between the shore and the boundary of the U.S. exclusive economic zone (200 nautical miles from shore). Note that in other documents, "coastal" may refer only to state waters, but in this report, the term "coastal waters" includes state and federally regulated waters.

[6] Although oil spills certainly occur in or reach non-coastal U.S. waters, this report focuses on issues and background information related to coastal water spills. However, in many cases, the issues overlap.

[7] NRC report, pp. 67-88.

[8] The NRC estimate for natural seep volume ranges from 24 million to 71 million gallons each year. The "best estimate" (included in **Figure 1**) is 47 million gallons (p. 69).

[9] NRC report, p. 2.

[10] This subcategory is particularly broad: municipal wastewaters, non-refinery industrial discharge, refinery discharges, urban runoff, river discharges, and ocean dumping.

[11] Includes large vessels, such as oil tankers, and smaller vessels, such as fishing boats.

[12] Includes motor boats, jet skis, and other recreational vessels.

[13] Atmospheric deposition generally refers to the process of air pollutants (generated from petroleum combustion) reaching water bodies through various mechanisms (e.g., precipitation). According to the NRC report, "atmospheric (continued...)

---

many of these sources are poorly understood. For example, oil from land-based sources—the largest estimated component of the consumption category—may not directly enter U.S. coastal waters until traveling through various man-made conveyances, such as storm-water drains. As such, the range of uncertainty of land-based runoff is substantial, from a minimum annual estimate of 5.6 million gallons to 588 million gallons.[14]

Figure 1. Estimates of Percentage Contribution of Oil into North American Coastal Waters, by Major Source Categories

Based on Average Annual Releases, 1990-1999

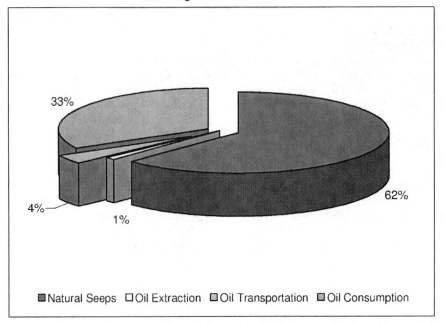

Source: Prepared by the Congressional Research Service (CRS) with data from the National Research Council (NRC) of the National Academies of Science, 2003, *Oil in the Sea III: Inputs, Fates, and Effects,* p. 69.

Notes: Extraction includes platform spills, produced waters, and atmospheric deposition. Transportation includes spills from tanker/barges, pipelines, coastal facilities, and atmospheric deposition. Oil consumption includes river and urban runoff, oil spills from cargo ships, operational discharges from commercial vessels and recreational craft, and atmospheric deposition. For further details of these inputs, see the NRC Report.

Potential Sources of Major Spills

Although oil transportation and oil extraction activities contribute (on average) a relatively small percentage of oil to U.S. waters (see **Figure 1**), sources within these sectors have generated major oil spills in U.S. coastal waters. Oil spill policy in the United States has generally focused on prevention, preparation, and response involving oil spills from these (and several other) sources.

(...continued)

deposition supplies hydrocarbons somewhat uniformly to the coastal ocean at relatively low loading rates over large areas" (p. 115).

[14] Based on average, annual releases from 1990-1999. NRC report, pp. 69, 87.

Figure 2 illustrates the combined number and volume of oil spills from selected sources, whose spills would likely impact U.S. coastal waters. These sources include oil tankers and barges, offshore platforms and pipelines, coastal facilities, and other vessels.[15] Prior to the 2010 Gulf spill, data between 1973 and 2007 indicate that both the number of spills and volume of oil entering U.S. coastal waters have declined; in some years, the declines have been dramatic.

This historical decline of *spill incidents* is likely related, at least in part, to international oil pollution standards that went into effect in 1983. These new standards were implemented in the United States by the Act to Prevent Pollution from Ships (discussed later in this report).[16]

Figure 3 compares the volume of spills over time from the same selected sources identified in **Figure 2**. As **Figure 3** illustrates, the primary source of oil spills in coastal waters has been oil tankers and barges. The substantial drop in the annual *spill volume* (illustrated in both figures) is most attributable to the decline in volume spilled by oil tankers and barges.

Figure 2. Annual Volume and Number of Oil Spills from Selected Sources
1973-2007

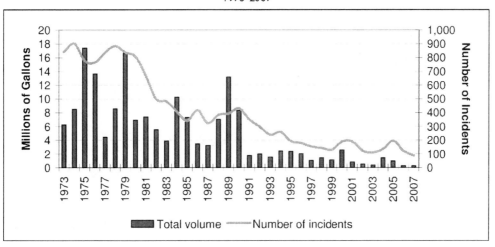

Source: Prepared by CRS; source data from Dagmar Etkin (Environmental Research Consulting), "40-Year Analysis of US Oil Spillage Rates," *Proceedings of the 33rd Arctic and Marine Oil Spill Program Technical Seminar on Environmental Contamination and Response.* Underlying data from various federal government agencies, including U.S. Coast Guard, Environmental Protection Agency, and Bureau of Ocean Energy Management, Regulation, and Enforcement (formerly the Minerals Management Service).

Notes: Sources include oil tankers and barges, coastal facilities, offshore platforms and pipelines, and other vessels. Other vessels includes spills from passenger vessels, fishing vessels, recreational vessels, unclassified vessels, and cargo ships. Spills from coastal facilities include some spills that may have been partially or completely captured by secondary containment structures. The number of incidents reflects data for tankers and barges, coastal facilities, offshore platforms and pipelines, and cargo ships.

---

[15] Other vessels includes spills from passenger vessels, fishing vessels, recreational vessels, unclassified vessels, and cargo ships. Cargo ships may carry oil for operational purposes (as opposed to tankers, which transport oil for commercial purposes). The volume stored on cargo ships can be substantial. For example, large container ships (e.g., the *Cosco Busan*, which spilled approximately 50,000 gallons in San Francisco Bay in 2007) may hold several million gallons of petroleum in multiple tanks.

[16] P.L. 96-478, 33 U.S.C. 1901 et seq. These standards and the U.S. law are discussed later in this report.

The volume of oil spilled from vessels in U.S. waters in the 1990s differed dramatically from the volume spilled in the 1980s. The *Exxon Valdez* spill of 1989 and the resulting Oil Pollution Act of 1990 (OPA) played key roles in the subsequent spill volume reduction. The 1990 Act (discussed below) made comprehensive changes to U.S. oil pollution law by expanding federal response authority and increasing spill liability. The high costs associated with the *Exxon Valdez* spill,[17] and the threat of broad liability imposed by OPA (in some scenarios, unlimited liability), have likely been the central drivers for the spill volume decline seen in the 1990s. In addition to international and federal governance, 28 states had oil spill liability laws, 19 of which imposed unlimited liability, before the *Exxon Valdez* spill occurred in 1989.[18] After the 1989 spill, some states enacted additional legislation,[19] which may have contributed to the declines.

Figure 3. Comparison of Estimated Oil Spill Volumes from Selected Sources

1973 - 2007

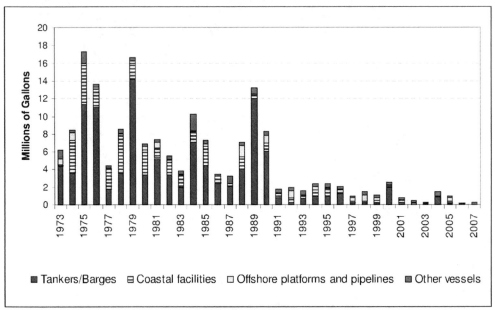

Source: Prepared by CRS; source data from Dagmar Etkin (Environmental Research Consulting), "40-Year Analysis of US Oil Spillage Rates," *Proceedings of the 33rd Arctic and Marine Oil Spill Program Technical Seminar on Environmental Contamination and Response.* Underlying data from various federal government agencies, including U.S. Coast Guard, Environmental Protection Agency, and Bureau of Ocean Energy Management, Regulation, and Enforcement (formerly the Minerals Management Service).

---

[17] The *Exxon Valdez* spill tallied approximately $2 billion in cleanup costs and $1 billion in natural resource damages (not including third-party claims)—in 1990 dollars. Punitive damage claims were litigated for more than 12 years, eventually reaching the U.S. Supreme Court in 2008 (*Exxon Shipping v. Baker*, 128 S. Ct. 2605 (2008)). Plaintiffs were eventually awarded approximately $500 million in punitive damages. An additional $500 million in interest on those damages was subsequently awarded.

[18] CRS Report (out-of-print, available from CRS by request), *Liability Provisions in State Oil Spill Laws: A Brief Summary,* October 1, 1990.

[19] For example, California passed the Lempert-Keene-Seastrand Oil Spill Prevention and Response Act in 1990. More information is available at http://www.dfg.ca.gov/ospr/about/history.html#.

Notes: Other vessels includes spills from passenger vessels, fishing vessels, recreational vessels, unclassified vessels, and cargo ships. Spills from coastal facilities include some spills that may have been partially or completely captured by secondary containment structures.

Although the volume of oil spills from oil tankers and barges has dwarfed other selected sources, the 2010 Gulf spill highlighted the worst-case discharge potential of spills from offshore oil extraction activities. Spills from offshore platforms and pipelines have typically represented (on an annual basis) only a relatively minor (only 0.05%) component of the total input to North American waters.[20] However, oil well blowouts from offshore oil extraction operations have historically been a source of major oil spills. Before the 2010 Gulf spill, the largest unintentional oil spill in world history—the *IXTOC I*, estimated at 140 million gallons—was due to an oil well blowout in Mexican Gulf Coast waters in 1979.[21] According to the federal government's estimate (from August 2, 2010), the 2010 Gulf spill eclipsed this volume by almost 50%. As a comparison, the largest oil tanker spill in world history—the *Atlantic Empress* off the coast of Tobago in 1979—was estimated at approximately 84 million gallons.[22]

Impacts of Oil Spills in Aquatic Environments

The impacts of an oil spill depend on the size of the spill, the rate of the spill, the type of oil spilled, and the location of the spill. Depending on timing and location, even a relatively minor spill can cause significant harm to individual organisms and entire populations.[23] Oil spills can cause impacts over a range of time scales, from days to years, or even decades for certain spills. Impacts are typically divided into acute (short-term) and chronic (long-term) effects. Both types are part of a complicated and often controversial equation that is addressed after an oil spill: ecosystem recovery.[24]

Acute Impacts

Depending on the toxicity and concentration of the spill, acute exposure to oil spills can kill various organisms and cause the following debilitating (but not necessarily lethal) effects:[25]

- reduced reproduction,
- altered development,
- impaired feeding mechanisms, and
- decreased defense from disease.

---

[20] While oil extraction activities contribute approximately 1% of the total oil input to North American waters, the vast majority (95%) of this (1%) oil extraction input comes from operational discharges, which are regulated by a Clean Water Act permit system. NRC Report, Table 3-2.

[21] NRC report, p. 33.

[22] For a list of the largest oil tanker spills, see The International Tanker Owners Pollution Federation (ITOPF) website, at http://www.itopf.com/.

[23] NRC report, p. 4.

[24] For additional information, see CRS Report R41311, *The Deepwater Horizon Oil Spill: Coastal Wetland and Wildlife Impacts and Response*, by M. Lynne Corn and Claudia Copeland.

[25] These "sub-lethal" effects can occur at concentrations that are several orders of magnitude lower than concentrations that cause death. NRC report, p. 127.

Birds, marine mammals, bottom-dwelling and intertidal species, and organisms in their developmental stages (e.g., fish eggs and larvae) are particularly vulnerable to oil spills.[26]

In addition to the impacts to individual organisms, oil spills can lead to a disruption of the structure and function of the ecosystem. Certain habitats—such as coral reefs, mangrove swamps, and salt marshes—are especially vulnerable, because the physical structure of the habitats depends upon living organisms.

These potential acute effects to individual organisms and marine ecosystems have been "unambiguously established" by laboratory studies and well-studied spills, such as the *Exxon Valdez*.[27]

Chronic Impacts

Long-term, chronic exposure typically occurs from continuous oil releases—leaking pipelines, offshore production discharges, and non-point sources (e.g., urban runoff). Although spills are normally associated with acute impacts, some oil spills have also demonstrated chronic exposure and effects.[28] There is increasing evidence that chronic, low-level exposures to oil contaminants can significantly affect the survival and reproductive success of marine birds and mammals.[29] However, because of the complexity of factors, including a longer time period and presence of other pollutants, determining the precise effects on species and ecosystems due to chronic oil exposure in a particular locale is difficult for scientists. As a result, studies involving chronic effects are often met with debate and some controversy.

Ecosystem Recovery

Interested parties may have differing opinions as to what constitutes ecosystem recovery. At one end of the spectrum, local groups may demand that an ecosystem be returned to pre-spill conditions. NOAA regulations (15 CFR Section 990.30) state that recovery "means the return of injured natural resources and services to baseline"—in other words, a return to conditions as they would have been had the spill not occurred. Baseline conditions may not equate with pre-spill conditions. Multiple variables affect local species and ecosystem services. For example, one species at a spill site could have been on the decline at the time of an incident, because of changing water temperatures. These types of trends are considered during the restoration evaluative process (discussed below). Restoration leaves room for site-specific interpretation, which, in the case of the *Exxon Valdez* spill and cleanup, continues to generate considerable argument.

---

[26] NRC report, Chapter 5; also multiple conversations with National Oceanic and Atmospheric Administration (NOAA) personnel (2008).

[27] NRC report, p. 120.

[28] NRC report, p. 121.

[29] NRC report, p. 134.

Economic Costs of Oil Spills

The economic costs that can result from an oil spill can be broken into three categories: cleanup expenses, natural resource damages, and the various economic losses incurred by the affected community or individuals.

Cleanup Costs

The cleanup costs of an oil spill can vary greatly and are influenced by a mix of factors: location characteristics, oil type, and oil volume.

Location

Location is generally considered the most important factor because it involves multiple variables. Areas with less water movement, such as marshlands, will generally cost more to clean up than open water. Some spill locations may have relatively robust populations of indigenous micro-organisms that help degrade the oil naturally.[30]

Tourist destinations or sensitive habitats, such as coral reefs, will likely require more stringent cleanup standards, thus increasing the costs. The political and social culture at the spill site plays a part as well. A spill in a high-profile area may receive special attention.[31] Major oil spills, especially ones that affect shoreline ecosystems, are often met with extensive media coverage, placing pressure on parties to take action. Coupled with this pressure, authorities (federal, state, or local) at these locations may require extensive oil spill response requirements, which can influence cleanup cost. For instance, spill costs in the United States are considerably higher than in other parts of the world.[32]

Oil Type

The more persistent and viscous oil types, such as heavy crude oil and intermediates known as bunker fuels, are more expensive to clean up. Gasoline and other lighter refined products may require only minimal cleanup action. Generally, these materials will evaporate or disperse relatively quickly, leaving only a small volume of petroleum product in the environment.

Oil Volume

Compared with other factors, spill volume is less important. A major spill away from shore will likely cost considerably less than a minor spill in a sensitive location. Certainly, the amount of oil

---

[30] See, for example, Terry Hazen et al., "Deep-Sea Plume Enriches Indigenous Oil-Degrading Bacteria," *Science* (Online), August 24, 2010; Richard Camilli et al., "Tracking Hydrocarbon Plume Transport and Biodegradation at *Deepwater Horizon*," *Science* (Online), August 19, 2010.

[31] For example, the November 7, 2007, spill (53,000 gallons) from a container ship into the San Francisco Bay generated considerable interest.

[32] The average cleanup cost is three times higher in the United States than in Europe (based on 1997 data and *excluding* the Exxon Valdez costs). See Etkin, Dagmar, "Estimating Cleanup Costs for Oil Spills," paper presented at the 1999 International Oil Spill Conference, 1999, citing data from the Oil Spill Intelligence Report International Oil Spill Database.

spilled affects cleanup costs, because, all things being equal, a larger spill will require a larger and more expensive cleanup effort. However, the relationship between cleanup costs and spill volume is not linear. Cleaning up a smaller spill is likely to cost more than a larger spill on a per-gallon basis.[33]

Natural Resources Damages

This category of costs relates to the environmental impacts caused by an oil spill. Pursuant to OPA, the party responsible for an oil spill is liable for any loss of natural resources (e.g., fish, animals, plants, and their habitats) and the services provided by the resource (e.g., drinking water, recreation).

When a spill occurs, natural resource trustees conduct a natural resource damage assessment to determine the extent of the harm. Trustees may include officials from federal agencies designated by the President, state agencies designated by the relevant governor, and representatives from tribal and foreign governments.[34] The various trustees assess damages to natural resources under their respective jurisdictions.[35] If multiple trustees are involved, they must select a lead administrative trustee (LAT), who coordinates trustee activities and serves as a liaison between oil spill responders. The LAT need not be from a federal agency; however, only a federal LAT can submit a request to the Oil Spill Liability Trust Fund for the initial assessment funding.[36]

The Oil Pollution Act (OPA) of 1990 states that the measure of natural resource damages includes

- the cost of restoring, rehabilitating, replacing, or acquiring the equivalent of the damaged natural resources;

- the diminution in value of those natural resources pending restoration; and

- the reasonable cost of assessing those damages.[37]

Pursuant to OPA, NOAA developed regulations pertaining to natural resource damage assessments in 1996.[38] Natural resource damages may include both losses of direct use and passive uses. Direct use value may derive from recreational (e.g., boating), commercial (e.g., fishing), or cultural or historical uses of the resource. In contrast, a passive-use value may derive from preserving the resource for its own sake or for enjoyment by future generations.[39]

---

[33] This is primarily due to the fact that a spill of any size (e.g., in a sensitive area) will require that equipment and response experts be sent to the scene. See Etkin, Dagmar, "Estimating Cleanup Costs for Oil Spills," paper presented at the 1999 International Oil Spill Conference, 1999, p. 5.

[34] For more information, see NOAA's Damage Assessment, Remediation, and Restoration Program at http://www.darrp.noaa.gov/about/index.html.

[35] 33 U.S.C. Section 2706(c). In some cases, trustees may share responsibility over the same resource. See, for example, Department of the Interior's "Pollution Response and Natural Resource Trusteeship Training Module On NRDA," at http://www.doi.gov/oepc/response/a01.htm.

[36] 33 U.S.C. Section 2712 and Executive Order (EO) 12777 (October 18, 1991).

[37] 33 U.S.C. Section 2706(d).

[38] 61 *Federal Register* 440 (January 5, 1996). See also NOAA, *Injury Assessment Guidance Document for Natural Resource Damage Assessment Under the Oil Pollution Act of 1990* (1996).

[39] See 15 CFR Section 990.30, definition of "value."

The damages are compensatory, not punitive. Collected damages cannot be placed into the general Treasury revenues of the federal or state government, but must be used to restore or replace lost resources.[40] Indeed, NOAA's regulations focus on the costs of primary restoration—returning the resource to its baseline condition—and compensatory restoration—addressing interim losses of resources and their services.[41]

Other Economic Costs

Oil spills can generate costs other than response expenses or damages to natural resources. An oil spill can disrupt business activity near the spill, particularly businesses and individuals that count on the resources and reputation of the local environment. For example, the local fishing and tourist industry may be affected. In some cases, a well-publicized oil spill can weaken local or regional industries near the spill site, regardless of the actual threat to human health created by the spill.

Local infrastructure and services can be disrupted by an oil spill. Port and harbor operations may be interrupted, altering the flow of trade goods. Power plants that use cooling water systems may need to temporarily cease operations. For example, the Salem Nuclear Plant—the second-largest nuclear plant in the United States—was forced to halt activity due to a substantial oil spill (more than 250,000 gallons) in the Delaware River in November 2004.

Unlike natural resource damage claims, which are brought by the appropriate natural resource trustees, the costs described in this section would be submitted as claims by the third parties suffering the specific loss.

Oil Spill Governance

When the *Exxon Valdez* ran aground in March 1989, there were multiple federal statutes, state statutes, and international conventions that dealt with oil discharges. The governing framework for oil spills in the United States remains a combination of federal, state, and international authorities. Within this framework, several federal agencies have the authority to implement oil spill regulations. The framework and primary federal funding process (the Oil Spill Liability Trust Fund) used to respond to oil spills are described below.

Federal Authorities: Before and After the *Exxon Valdez* Spill

The following list highlights the primary federal authorities that were in effect when the *Exxon Valdez* spill occurred in 1989:

- Clean Water Act (1972):[42] The Clean Water Act (CWA) represented the broadest authority for addressing oil spills at the time of the *Exxon Valdez* spill. Section

---

[40] 33 U.S.C. Section 2706(f); William D. Brighton, *Natural Resource Damages under the Comprehensive Environmental Response, Compensation, and Liability Act* (2006), U.S. Department of Justice, Environment and Natural Resources Division.

[41] William D. Brighton, *Natural Resource Damages under the Comprehensive Environmental Response, Compensation, and Liability Act* (2006), U.S. Department of Justice, Environment and Natural Resources Division.

[42] The official statutory name is the Federal Water Pollution Control Act, P.L. 92-500, as amended, codified at 33 (continued...)

311 of the CWA established requirements for oil spill reporting, response, and liability. The act also created a fund (311 Fund), maintained by federal appropriations, that could be used for cleanup and natural resource restoration.

- Deepwater Port Act (1974):[43] This statute addressed oil spills and liability issues at deepwater oil ports. The act also set up the Deepwater Port Fund to provide for prompt cleanup and to compensate damages above liability limits. The fund was financed by a per-gallon tax on oil transferred at a deepwater port.

- Trans-Alaska Pipeline Authorization Act (1973):[44] This act covered oil spills and liability relating to the Trans-Alaska Pipeline System (TAPS). Although the pipeline is constructed over land, spills from it could reach coastal waters via inland rivers. The act created a trust fund, financed through a lessee fee, that could be used to respond to spills and damages from the pipeline.

- Outer Continental Shelf Lands Act Amendments (1978):[45] This act established an oil spill liability structure and rules for oil extraction facilities in federal offshore waters. With this legislation, Congress created the Offshore Pollution Fund, financed by a per-gallon fee on produced oil, that could be used for oil spill cleanup and damages.

- National Oil and Hazardous Substances Pollution Contingency Plan (NCP): The first NCP was administratively prepared in 1968 after observing the British government's response to a 37-million-gallon oil tanker spill (*Torrey Canyon*) off the coast of England.[46] The NCP contains the federal government's procedures for responding to oil spills and hazardous substance releases.[47] (The NCP is discussed in more detail later in this report.)

After the *Exxon Valdez* spill, many observers[48] described the above legal collection as an ineffective patchwork. Arguably, each law had perceived shortcomings (discussed below in the context of post-*Exxon Valdez* legislation), and none provided comprehensive oil spill coverage.

For more than 15 years prior to the *Exxon Valdez* incident, Congress made attempts to enact a unified oil pollution law. Several contentious issues produced deadlocks, hindering the passage of legislation. One of the central points of debate, state preemption, dealt with whether a federal oil spill law should limit a state's ability to impose stricter requirements, particularly unlimited liability. Other liability questions also generated debate. For example, if an oil spill occurred, should the owner of the cargo (i.e., oil) be held liable, as was the ship owner/operator? Another point of contention was whether oil-carrying vessels should be required to have double hulls. Although proponents argued that a second hull would help prevent oil spills, the shipping

---

(...continued)

U.S.C. 1251 et seq.

[43] P.L. 93-627, codified at 33 U.S.C. 1501 et seq.

[44] P.L. 93-153, codified at 43 U.S.C. 1651 et seq.

[45] P.L. 95-372, codified at 43 U.S.C. 1801 et seq.

[46] See EPA "National Contingency Plan Overview" at http://www.epa.gov/emergencies/content/lawsregs/ncpover.htm.

[47] The NCP is codified at 40 CFR Part 300.

[48] See, for example, U.S. Congress, House Committee on Merchant Marine and Fisheries, Report accompanying H.R. 1465, Oil Pollution Prevention, Removal, Liability, and Compensation Act of 1989, 1989, H.Rept. 101-242, Part 2, 101st Cong., 1st sess., p. 32.

industry raised concern that implementing such a mandate would disrupt oil transportation and potentially affect the national economy. A final issue involved the interaction between domestic legislation (federal and state) and international measures. Some were concerned that if the United States became a party to certain international agreements under consideration in the 1980s,[49] the international standards would preempt federal and state laws, especially those establishing liability limits. Proponents argued that these concerns were overstated and stressed that joining the international agreements was especially important for the United States because of the international nature of oil transportation and associated pollution.

Following the 1989 *Exxon Valdez* spill, Members of Congress faced great pressure to overcome the disputes discussed above.[50] The spill highlighted the inadequacies of the existing coverage and generated public outrage. The end result was the Oil Pollution Act of 1990 (OPA)[51]—the first comprehensive law to specifically address oil pollution to waterways and coastlines of the United States.

Oil Pollution Act of 1990

With the enactment of OPA on August 18, 1990, Congress consolidated the existing federal oil spill laws under one program. The 1990 law expanded the existing liability provisions within the CWA and created new free-standing requirements regarding oil spill prevention and response. Key OPA provisions are discussed below.

Spill Response Authority

When responding to a spill, many considered the lines of responsibility under the pre-OPA regime to be unclear,[52] with too much reliance on spillers to perform proper cleanup.[53] OPA strengthened and clarified the federal government's role in oil spill response and cleanup. OPA Section 4201 amended Section 311(c) of the CWA to provide the President (delegated to the U.S. Coast Guard or EPA) with authority to perform cleanup immediately using federal resources,[54] monitor the response efforts of the spiller, or direct the spiller's cleanup activities. The revised response authorities addressed concerns "that precious time would be lost while waiting for the spiller to marshall its cleanup forces."[55]

The federal government—specifically the On-Scene Coordinator (OSC) for spills in the Coast Guard's jurisdiction—determines the level of cleanup required. Although the federal government

---

[49] The two agreements under consideration were the 1984 Protocols to the International Convention on Civil Liability for Oil Pollution Damage and the Protocols to the International Fund for Compensation for Oil Pollution Damages.

[50] A handful of other oil spills followed the *Exxon Valdez* in 1989 and 1990 (e.g., the *Mega Borg* spilled 5 million gallons of oil in the Gulf of Mexico), further spurring congressional action.

[51] P.L. 101-380, primarily codified at U.S.C. 2701 et seq.

[52] See, for example, Wilkinson, Cynthia et al., "Slick Work: An Analysis of the Oil Pollution Act of 1990," *Journal of Energy, Natural Resources, and Environmental Law*, 12 (1992), p. 190.

[53] See Grumbles, Benjamin, and Manley, Joan, "The Oil Pollution Act of 1990: Legislation in the Wake of a Crisis," *Natural Resources and Environment*, 10:2 (1995), p. 38.

[54] Leading up to the passage of OPA, parties referred to this approach as "federalizing" the spill.

[55] U.S. Congress, House Committee on Merchant Marine and Fisheries, Report accompanying H.R. 1465, Oil Pollution Prevention, Removal, Liability, and Compensation Act of 1989, 1989, H.Rept. 101-242, Part 2, 101st Cong., 1st sess., p. 84.

must consult with designated trustees of natural resources and the governor of the state affected by the spill, the decision that cleanup is completed and can be ended rests with the federal government. States may require further work, but without the support of federal funding.[56]

National Contingency Plan

OPA expanded the role and breadth of the NCP. The 1990 law established a multi-layered planning and response system to improve preparedness and response to spills in marine environments.[57] Among other things, the act also required the President to establish procedures and standards (as part of the NCP) for responding to worst-case oil spill scenarios.[58]

Tank Vessel and Facility Response Plans

As a component of the enhanced NCP, OPA amended the CWA to require that U.S. tank vessels, offshore facilities, and certain onshore facilities[59] prepare and submit oil spill response plans to the relevant federal agency. In general, vessels and facilities are prohibited from handling, storing, or transporting oil if they do not have a plan approved by (or submitted to) the appropriate agency (discussed below).[60]

The plans should, among other things, identify how the owner or operator of a vessel or facility would respond to a worst-case scenario spill. Congress did not intend for every vessel to have onboard all the personnel and equipment needed to respond to a worst-case spill, but vessels must have a plan and procedures to call upon—typically through a contractual relationship—the necessary equipment and personnel for responding to a worst-case spill.[61]

In 2004, Congress enacted an amendment requiring non-tank vessels (i.e., ships carrying oil for their own fuel use) over 400 gross tons to prepare and submit a vessel response plan.[62] Congress reasoned that many non-tank vessels have as much oil onboard as small tank vessels, thus presenting a comparable risk from an oil spill. Moreover, the international standards for oil spill prevention[63] apply to tanker and non-tanker vessels alike. Thus, the 2004 amendment brought the U.S. law more in line with international provisions.

---

[56] OPA Section 1011.

[57] OPA Section 4202, amending Section 311(j) of the CWA.

[58] OPA Section 4201(b), amending Section 311(d)(2)(J) of the CWA.

[59] The response plan requirement is applicable only to an onshore facility that, because of its location, could reasonably be expected to cause substantial harm to the environment by discharging into navigable waters, adjoining shorelines, or the exclusive economic zone. CWA Section 311(j)(5)(iii).

[60] OPA Section 4202, amending Section 311(j)(5)(E) of the CWA.

[61] U.S. Congress, House Committee on Merchant Marine and Fisheries, Report accompanying H.R. 1465, Oil Pollution Prevention, Removal, Liability, and Compensation Act of 1989, 1989, H.Rept. 101-242, Part 2, 101st Cong., 1st sess., p. 87. OPA Section 4202, amending Section 311(j)(5)(C)(iii) of the CWA.

[62] Amendments Relating to the Oil Pollution Act of 1990, Title VII of Coast Guard and Maritime Transportation Act of 2004 (P.L. 108-293), codified at 33 U.S.C. 1321.

[63] Primarily the shipboard oil pollution emergency plans required by MARPOL 73/78, discussed later in this report.

Double-Hull Design for Vessels

The issue of double hulls received considerable debate for many years prior to OPA, and it was one of the stumbling blocks for unified oil spill legislation. Proponents maintained that double-hull construction provides extra protection if a vessel becomes damaged.[64] However, opponents argued that a double-hulled vessel might cause stability problems if an accident occurred, thus negating the benefits.[65] Stakeholders also highlighted the impacts that a double-hull requirement would entail for the shipping industry (e.g., cost and time of retrofitting, ship availability).[66] The OPA requirements for double hulls reflected some of these concerns.

The act required new vessels carrying oil and operating in U.S. waters to have double hulls.[67] However, OPA provided certain exceptions, depending on the size of the vessel (e.g., less than 5,000 gross tons)[68] and its particular use (e.g., lightering).[69] For older vessels, OPA established a staggered retrofitting schedule, based on vessel age and size. As of January 2010, single-hull vessels (with several exceptions, some of which expire in 2015) cannot operate in U.S. waters.

Liability Issues

OPA unified the liability provisions of existing oil spill statutes, creating a freestanding liability regime. Section 1002 states that responsible parties are liable for any discharge of oil (or threat of discharge) from a vessel or facility[70] to navigable waters, adjoining shorelines, or the exclusive economic zone[71] of the United States (i.e., 200 nautical miles beyond the shore).

Regarding the oil spill statutes prior to OPA, Congress recognized that "there is no comprehensive legislation in place that promptly and adequately compensates those who suffer other types of economic loss as a result of an oil pollution incident."[72] OPA broadened the scope of damages (i.e., costs) for which an oil spiller would be liable. Under OPA, a responsible party is liable for all cleanup costs incurred, not only by a government entity, but also by a private party.[73]

---

[64] A study from the National Academy of Sciences reached this conclusion in 1999. See National Research Council, *Double hull Tanker Legislation: An Assessment of the Oil Pollution Act of 1990*, National Academies of Science, 1999, p. 144.

[65] Opponents maintained that if water entered the space between hulls, the ship could become unstable, hindering salvage and possibly capsizing. Cynthia Wilkinson et al., "Slick Work: An Analysis of the Oil Pollution Act of 1990," *Journal of Energy, Natural Resources, and Environmental Law*, 12 (1992), p. 196.

[66] U.S. Congress, Conference Report accompanying H.R. 1465, Oil Pollution Act of 1990, H. Conf. Rept. 101-653, at 140-141 (1990).

[67] OPA Section 4115, amending 46 U.S.C. 3703.

[68] This exception applied to many inland barges.

[69] Lightering is the process of transferring oil from a large vessel to a smaller vessel. This common practice occurs in designated areas that are typically many miles away from shore.

[70] The definition of "facility" is broadly worded and includes pipelines and motor vehicles. OPA Section 1001.

[71] Under the pre-OPA regime (primarily the CWA), a discharge 12 miles beyond shore had to affect the natural resources before liability attached. Under OPA Section 1002, the discharge itself triggers liability. Cynthia Wilkinson et al., "Slick Work: An Analysis of the Oil Pollution Act of 1990," *Journal of Energy, Natural Resources, and Environmental Law*, 12 (1992), p. 201.

[72] U.S. Congress, House Committee on Merchant Marine and Fisheries, Report accompanying H.R. 1465, Oil Pollution Prevention, Removal, Liability, and Compensation Act of 1989, 1989, H.Rept. 101-242, Part 2, 101st Cong., 1st sess., p. 31.

[73] OPA Section 1002(b)(1).

In addition to cleanup costs, OPA significantly increased the range of liable damages to include the following:

- injury to natural resources,

- loss of personal property (and resultant economic losses),

- loss of subsistence use of natural resources,

- lost revenues resulting from destruction of property or natural resource injury,

- lost profits and earning capacity resulting from property injury or natural resource injury, and

- costs of providing extra public services during or after spill response.[74]

OPA provided limited defenses from liability: act of God, act of war, and act or omission of certain third parties. These defenses are similar to those of the Superfund statute,[75] established in 1980 for releases of hazardous substances (which does not include oil).

Except for certain behavior, including acts of gross negligence or willful misconduct,[76] OPA set liability limits (or caps) for cleanup costs and other damages. Until 2006, liability limits for vessels were based on vessel carrying capacity, generally $1,200 per gross ton. As an example, the liability limit for the 2004 *Athos* tanker spill in Delaware River was approximately $45 million.[77]

OPA requires the President to issue regulations to adjust the liability limits at least every three years to take into account changes in the consumer price index (CPI). Despite this requirement, adjustments to liability limits were not made until Congress amended OPA in July 2006. The Coast Guard and Maritime Transportation Act of 2006 (P.L. 109-241) increased limits to $1,900/gross ton for double-hulled vessels and $3,000/gross ton for single-hulled vessels. Furthermore, the Coast Guard made its first CPI adjustment to the liability limits in 2009, increasing the limits to $2,000 and $3,200, respectively.[78]

Mobile offshore drilling units (MODUs), like the *Deepwater Horizon* unit involved in the April 2010 incident in the Gulf of Mexico, are first treated as tank vessels for their liability cap. If removal and damage costs exceed this liability cap, a MODU is deemed to be an offshore facility for the excess amount.[79]

---

[74] OPA Section 1002(b)(2).

[75] Section 107(b) of the Comprehensive Environmental Response, Compensation, and Liability Act (CERCLA, commonly known as Superfund), P.L. 96-510.

[76] In addition, liability limits are unavailable if the violation of a federal safety, construction, or operating requirement proximately caused the spill. Spillers must also report the incident and cooperate with response officials to take advantage of the liability caps. OPA Section 1004(c).

[77] 37,895 gross tons x $1,200/ton = $45.47 million. Vessel data from United States Coast Guard, *Investigation into the Striking of Submerged Objects by the Tank Vessel Athos I in the Delaware River on November 26, 2004 with a Major Discharge of Oil*, January 2006, p. 4.

[78] U.S. Coast Guard, "Consumer Price Index Adjustments of Oil Pollution Act of 1990 Limits of Liability—Vessels and Deepwater Ports," *Federal Register* Volume 74, No. 125 (July 1, 2009), pp. 31357-31369.

[79] 33 USC 2704(b).

Offshore facility liability is unlimited for removal costs but capped at $75 million for other costs and damages; onshore facility and deepwater port liability is limited to $350 million. In contrast to tank vessel liability limits, these liability limits are at the same level as they were in 1990.

The Oil Spill Liability Trust Fund

Prior to OPA, federal funding for oil spill response was generally considered inadequate,[80] and damages recovery was difficult for private parties.[81] To help address these issues, Congress supplemented OPA's expanded range of covered damages with the Oil Spill Liability Trust Fund (OSLTF).

Pursuant to Executive Order (EO) 12777, the Coast Guard created the National Pollution Funds Center (NPFC) to manage the trust fund in 1991. The fund may be used for several purposes:

- prompt payment of costs for responding to and removing oil spills;

- payment of the costs incurred by the federal and state trustees of natural resources for assessing the injuries to natural resources caused by an oil spill, and developing and implementing the plans to restore or replace the injured natural resources;

- payment of parties' claims for uncompensated removal costs, and for uncompensated damages (e.g., financial losses of fishermen, hotels, and beachfront businesses);

- payment for the net loss of government revenue, and for increased public services by a state or its political subdivisions; and

- payment of federal administrative and operational costs, including research and development, and $25 million per year for the Coast Guard's operating expenses.

Although Congress created the OSLTF in 1986,[82] Congress did not authorize its use or provide its funding until after the *Exxon Valdez* incident. In 1990, OPA provided the statutory authorization necessary to put the fund in motion. Through OPA, Congress transferred balances from other federal liability funds[83] into the OSLTF. In complementary legislation, Congress imposed a 5-cent-per-barrel tax on the oil industry to support the fund.[84] Collection of this fee ceased on December 31, 1994, due to a sunset provision in the law. However, in April 2006, the tax resumed as required by the Energy Policy Act of 2005 (P.L. 109-58). In addition, the Emergency Economic

---

[80] Wilkinson, Cynthia et al., "Slick Work: An Analysis of the Oil Pollution Act of 1990," *Journal of Energy, Natural Resources, and Environmental Law,* 12 (1992), p. 188.

[81] U.S. Congress, House Committee on Merchant Marine and Fisheries, Report accompanying H.R. 1465, Oil Pollution Prevention, Removal, Liability, and Compensation Act of 1989, 1989, H.Rept. 101-242, Part 2, 101st Cong., 1st sess., p. 35.

[82] Omnibus Budget Reconciliation Act of 1986 (P.L. 99-509).

[83] The CWA Section 311(k) revolving fund; the Deepwater Port Liability Fund; the Trans-Alaska Pipeline Liability Fund; and the Offshore Oil Pollution Compensation Fund.

[84] Omnibus Budget Reconciliation Act of 1989 (P.L. 101-239). Other revenue sources for the fund include interest on the fund, cost recovery from the parties responsible for the spills, and any fines or civil penalties collected.

Stabilization Act of 2008 (P.L. 110-343) increased the tax rate to 8 cents through 2016. In 2017, the rate increases to 9 cents. The tax is scheduled to terminate at the end of 2017.[85]

Financial Responsibility

To preserve the trust fund and ensure that responsible parties can be held accountable for oil spill cleanup and damages, OPA requires that vessels and offshore facilities maintain evidence of financial responsibility (e.g., insurance). The Coast Guard's National Pollution Funds Center (NPFC) implements the financial responsibility provisions for vessels; the Bureau of Ocean Energy Management, Regulation, and Enforcement (formerly the Minerals Management Service, MMS) implements this requirement for offshore facilities.

The current levels of financial responsibility are related to the current liability limits for various sources (e.g., vessels, offshore facilities) of potential oil spills. The liability limits differ by potential source. In the case of vessels, whose liability limits are a single dollar amount encompassing both removal costs and other damages, the financial responsibility levels are directly tied to the corresponding liability caps. Current law requires responsible parties for vessels to demonstrate the "maximum amount of liability to which the responsible party could be subjected under [the liability limits in OPA Section 1004; 33 U.S.C. 2704]."

Because the structure of offshore facility liability limit is different than vessels, the corresponding financial responsibility limit provisions differ. Responsible parties for offshore facilities in federal waters must demonstrate $35 million financial responsibility, unless the President determines a greater amount (not to exceed $150 million) is justified (33 U.S.C. 2716(c)). The federal regulations that are authored by this statutory provision (30 CFR Part 254) base the financial responsibility amount—between $35 million and $150 million—on a facility's worst-case discharge volume (as defined in 30 CFR Section 253.14). For example, a facility with a worst-case discharge volume over 105,000 barrels[86]—the highest level of worst-case discharge listed in the regulations—must maintain $150 million in financial responsibility.

Other Federal Laws

Although OPA is the primary domestic legislation for oil spills, other federal laws contain provisions that relate to oil spills. Many of these provisions were in place before OPA. The following list is not all-inclusive, but it highlights the main requirements authorized by laws other than OPA.

Clean Water Act

The Clean Water Act (CWA) was the primary federal statute governing oil spills prior to OPA and many provisions continue to apply. A key provision is found in Section 311(b)(3), which prohibits the discharge of oil or hazardous substances into U.S. navigable waters. In addition, the CWA

---

[85] Section 405 of P.L. 110-343.

[86] This amount is significantly less than the 4.9 million barrels estimated to have been released during the 2010 Gulf spill. See National Incident Command's Flow Rate Technical Group, press release, August 2, 2010.

contains various penalty provisions for noncompliance, including violations of the discharge prohibition of Section 311(b).[87]

Pursuant to statutory requirements in the CWA,[88] the EPA crafted regulations[89] for spill prevention control and countermeasure (SPCC) plans in 1973. SPCC plans address the "procedures, methods, and equipment and other requirements for equipment to prevent discharges."[90] The EPA's SPCC plans apply only to non-transportation, onshore facilities that exceed a certain oil storage capacity and that, in the event of a spill, can be reasonably expected, because of their location, to produce an oil discharge that would reach navigable waters or adjoining shorelines of the United States.[91] Unlike other oil spill preparedness provisions, SPCC plans focus more on prevention than on response activities, requiring, for example, secondary containment (e.g., dikes, berms) for oil-storage equipment.

The agency offered several regulatory amendments after the 1973 rulemaking. Following the passage of the Oil Pollution Act of 1990 (OPA),[92] the agency proposed substantial changes and clarifications that were not made final until July 2002. For reasons beyond the scope of this report, the effective date of the 2002 final rule has been extended multiple times; for some parts of the amended rule, the current effective date was January 14, 2009, and for other parts, the effective date was extended to November 10, 2010.[93] However, EPA proposed in July 2010 to extend the date an additional year for most facilities.[94]

Outer Continental Shelf Lands Act

The primary federal law governing oil development and operations in waters in federal jurisdiction is the Outer Continental Shelf Lands Act (OCSLA) of 1953 and its subsequent amendments (43 U.S.C. §§ 1331-1356). The OCSLA provided the foundation for regulations (30 CFR Part 250) that are implemented by the Bureau of Ocean Energy Management, Regulation, and Enforcement (formerly the Minerals Management Service, MMS). Sections of these regulations address oil spill prevention and response issues by requiring that various equipment and procedures be in place at offshore facilities.[95]

---

[87] For further discussion, see CRS Report R41370, *Federal Civil and Criminal Penalties Possibly Applicable to Parties Responsible for the Gulf of Mexico Oil Spill*, by Robert Meltz.

[88] Section 311(j)(1) of the 1972 CWA called for regulations to prevent the discharge of oil from vessels, onshore facilities, and offshore facilities. Executive Order 11735 (August 3, 1973) granted EPA the authority to regulate non-transportation-related onshore and offshore facilities.

[89] U.S. EPA, "Oil Pollution Prevention: Non-Transportation Related Onshore and Offshore Facilities," *Federal Register*, vol. 38, no. 237 (December 11, 1973), pp. 34164-34170.

[90] CWA Section 311(j)(1)(C).

[91] See 40 CFR Section 112.1.

[92] P.L. 101-380, primarily codified at U.S.C. 2701 et seq.

[93] For a comprehensive history of the regulations, see *Federal Register*, vol. 74, pp. 58784 (November 13, 2009).

[94] For more information, see EPA's SPCC website at http://www.epa.gov/emergencies/content/spcc/index.htm.

[95] For more information, see CRS Report RL33404, *Offshore Oil and Gas Development: Legal Framework*, by Adam Vann.

Pipeline Legislation

The U.S. pipeline network is extensive. Recent estimates indicate there are more than 33,000 miles of pipelines just in the Gulf of Mexico.[96] Moreover, U.S. inland pipelines are concentrated in coastal areas, particularly in the Gulf states, and these pipelines may have an impact on coastal waters if spills reach waterways that empty into coastal waters.

Several laws govern oil pipelines. The Hazardous Liquid Pipeline Act of 1979 (P.L. 96-129) granted authority to the Department of Transportation (DOT) to regulate various issues regarding oil spills from pipelines. On December 29, 2006, the President signed the Pipeline Safety Improvement Act of 2006 (P.L. 109-468) to improve pipeline safety and security practices, and to reauthorize the federal Office of Pipeline Safety.[97] The Office of Pipeline Safety (OPS), which is part of the DOT, implements provisions concerning pipeline design, construction, operation and maintenance, and spill response planning.[98]

July 2010 Pipeline Oil Spill into the Kalamazoo River

On July 26, 2010, a pipeline released approximately 800,000 gallons of crude oil of oil into Michigan's Talmadge Creek, a waterway that flows into the Kalamazoo River. As the federal OSC (for the inland zone), EPA established a Unified Command of federal, state and local agencies, and private parties to respond to the spill. Pursuant to the liability provisions in OPA, Enbridge Energy Partners, LLP is the responsible party for the spill.

For more up-to-date information, see EPA's Enbridge oil spill website, at http://www.epa.gov/enbridgespill/index.html.

Vessel Legislation

Several federal laws directly or indirectly deal with oil pollution from vessels.[99] Laws concerning navigation reduce the possibilities of vessel collision or hull breach by objects in the waterways.[100] Other laws call for particular vessel design standards. For example, the Ports and Waterways Safety Act of 1972,[101] amended by the Port and Tanker Safety Act of 1978,[102] called for specific construction and equipment design requirements for oil tankers. (As noted, OPA subsequently amended this statute in 1990 to establish a phased-in schedule for double-hulled tankers.) Congress enacted the 1970s legislation to coincide with international initiatives. In fact, many of the federal laws concerning vessel standards and pollution control procedures were written to implement international conventions. These laws are discussed in the next section.

---

[96] See, for example, MMS Press Release from February 2, 2005, at http://www.mms.gov/ooc/press/2005/press0202.htm.

[97] See 49 U.S.C. 60101 et seq.

[98] For further information on pipeline legislation, see CRS Report RL33347, *Pipeline Safety and Security: Federal Programs*, by Paul W. Parfomak.

[99] For a comprehensive list of federal maritime legislation see USCG, *Marine Safety Manual*, Vol. IX (undated), Chapter 1, available at http://homeport.uscg.mil.

[100] For example, the Rivers and Harbors Act of 1899, as amended (33 U.S.C. 401 et seq.), and the International Regulations for Preventing Collisions at Sea, as amended (33 U.S.C. 1601 et seq.).

[101] P.L. 92-340, 33 U.S.C. 1221 et seq.

[102] P.L. 95-474, codified at 33 U.S.C. 1221-1232 and 46 U.S.C. 3701-3718.

Federal Agencies' Responsibilities

The United States shares jurisdiction over its coastal waters with the coastal states. The 1953 Submerged Lands Act (SLA) gave coastal states jurisdiction over the submerged lands, waters, and natural resources (e.g., oil deposits) located, in most cases, within 3 nautical miles off the coastline.[103] The waters, seabed, and natural resources beyond the states' waters are exclusively federal, and extend to the edge of the exclusive economic zone (200 nautical miles from shore). However, the federal government maintains the authority to regulate commerce, navigation, national defense, power production, and international affairs within state waters.

The oil spill legal framework involves implementation by multiple federal agencies. Agency responsibilities can be divided into two categories: (1) oil spill response and cleanup and (2) oil spill prevention/preparedness.

Response

As mentioned above, the National Oil and Hazardous Substances Pollution Contingency Plan (NCP) contains the federal government's framework and operative requirements for responding to an oil spill (and releases of hazardous substances). Although first developed through administrative processes in 1968, subsequent laws have amended the NCP, including the Clean Water Act in 1972; the Comprehensive Environmental Response, Compensation, and Liability Act (CERCLA or Superfund) in 1980; and the Oil Pollution Act (OPA) in 1990. Oil spill response actions required under the regulations of the NCP are binding and enforceable, per these enforcement authorities.

The NCP establishes the National Response System (NRS), a multi-tiered and coordinated national response strategy for addressing oil spills and releases of hazardous substances. The NCP provisions specific to oil spill response are codified in 40 C.F.R. Part 300, Subpart D. Key components of the NRS include the following:

- National Response Team (NRT): composed of representatives from the federal departments and agencies assigned roles in responding to oil spills. The U.S. Coast Guard chairs the NRT when a response is being mounted to a spill in a coastal region.

- Regional Response Teams (RRTs): composed of regional representatives of each NRT member agency, state governments, and local governments. The Coast Guard leads the relevant RRT during responses to oil spills in coastal waters.

- Area Committees (ACs): composed of qualified personnel from federal, state, and local agencies. The primary function of each AC is to prepare an Area Contingency Plan (ACP) for its designated area.

- On-Scene Coordinator (OSC): who directs the response efforts and coordinates all other efforts at the scene.

---

[103] Most state waters extend 3 nautical miles (1 nautical mile = 6,076 feet, or 1.15 miles) from shore. Louisiana waters extend 3 imperial nautical miles (1 imperial nautical mile = 6,080 feet). Texas and Gulf Coast of Florida waters extend 3 marine leagues (equating to 9 nautical miles). See the MMS, OCS, website ("Definitions and Jurisdictions") at http://www.mms.gov/incidents/pollution.htm. See also CRS Report RL33404, *Offshore Oil and Gas Development: Legal Framework*, by Adam Vann.

Oil spill response authority is determined by the location of the spill: the Coast Guard has response authority in the coastal zone, and the EPA covers the inland zone.[104] The OSC has the ultimate authority to ensure that an oil spill is effectively removed and actions are taken to prevent further discharge from the source. The OSC is broadly empowered to direct and coordinate all response and recovery activities of federal, state, local, and private entities (including the responsible party), and will draw on resources available through the appropriate ACPs and RRTs.

Although the OSC must consult with designated trustees of natural resources and the governor of the state affected by the spill, the OSC has the authority and responsibility to determine when removal (i.e., cleanup) is complete.

Other agencies, particularly those on the NRT and relevant RRT, may play a role in response activities. As the chair of the NRT (and vice-chair during oil spills in the coastal zone), EPA may provide response support. For example, during the *Deepwater Horizon* spill response, EPA conducted air and water sampling and provided environmental monitoring support, particularly regarding the use of dispersants.

In addition, NOAA provides scientific analysis and consultation during oil spill response activities.[105] Assistance can include oil spill tracking, cleanup alternatives, and knowledge of at-risk natural resources. Moreover, NOAA experts begin to collect data to assess natural resource damages during response operations.

Prevention and Preparedness

Regarding oil spill prevention and preparedness duties, jurisdiction is determined by the potential sources (e.g., vessels, facilities, pipelines) of oil spills. A series of executive orders (EOs), coupled with memoranda of understanding (MOU), have established the various agency responsibilities.[106] **Table 1** identifies the agencies responsible for implementing prevention and preparedness regulations for the potential sources of oil spills.

---

[104] The terms inland zone and coastal zone are defined in the National Contingency Plan (40 CFR Section 300.5). The coastal zone covers all waters subject to the tide, the Great Lakes, and all seaward waters (extending 200 nautical miles beyond shore). The inland zone covers all other U.S. waters. Spills in inland waters can potentially affect coastal waters and ecosystems, particularly if the spill occurs in water systems near the coast. In fact, a fine line may separate specific inland and coastal waters (e.g., consider the nexus between a bay and a river).

[105] For more information see NOAA's Office of Response and Restoration website, at http://response.restoration.noaa.gov/index.php.

[106] Executive Order (EO) 12777 (October 18, 1991) delegates authorities pursuant to the Oil Pollution Act of 1990. This order was amended by EO 13286 (March 5, 2003), which reorganized duties in response to the creation of the Department of Homeland Security.

**Table 1. Federal Agency Jurisdiction for Oil Spill Prevention
and Preparedness Duties, by Source**

Potential Source of Oil Spill	Responsible Agency
Vessels	Coast Guard
Onshore, non-transportation facilities	EPA
Onshore, transportation facilities	Coast Guard and Department of Transportation (DOT)
Deepwater ports[a]	Coast Guard and DOT
Offshore facilities (oil/gas extraction)	Bureau of Ocean Energy Management, Regulation, and Enforcement (formerly the Minerals Management Service, MMS) within the Department of Interior
Offshore pipelines directly associated with oil extraction activities (i.e., "production lines")[b]	Bureau of Ocean Energy Management, Regulation, and Enforcement (formerly the Minerals Management Service, MMS) within the Department of Interior
Offshore pipelines *not* directly associated with oil extraction activities (i.e., "transmission lines")	Office of Pipeline Safety (OPS) within the DOT
Inland pipelines	OPS

a. There is only one deepwater port for oil in U.S. coastal waters: the Louisiana Offshore Oil Port (LOOP).

b. For further discussion on federal pipeline jurisdiction, see National Research Council, *Improving the Safety of Marine Pipelines*, National Academies of Science, 1994, pp. 86-89.

Prevention responsibilities include, among other things, assessing whether facilities or vessels have the necessary equipment in place. As discussed above, vessels may be required to have double hulls; facilities may need secondary containment.

Preparedness duties involve oversight tasks, such as evaluating facility and vessel response plans. Preparedness responsibilities also include developing and maintaining contingency plans at various levels: area, regional, and national. Personnel training is a vital component of sustaining readiness. NOAA oil spill experts help train responders in government service and private business.

In addition, OPA requires agencies to conduct internal examinations to test preparedness.[107] As part of this requirement, the Coast Guard conducts Spills of National Significance (SONS) exercises to analyze the Coast Guard's ability to respond to a major oil spill.

International Conventions

The relationship between international and domestic law can be complex. For example, a "self-executing" agreement taking the form of a treaty, signed by the Executive and ratified with the advice and consent of the Senate, stands on equal footing with federal statute. On the other hand, if an international agreement is not self-executing, implementing legislation may be necessary for the agreement's provisions to be given domestic legal effect, including to provide U.S. agencies with the domestic legal authority necessary to carry out functions contemplated under the

---

[107] As required by OPA Section 4202(a), which amended CWA Section 311(j)(7), codified in 33 U.S.C. 1321(j)(7).

agreement. Several federal laws governing oil spills were fashioned to implement obligations contained in international agreements.[108]

International conventions have played an important role in developing consistent standards for oil-carrying vessels from different nations. A primary player in this regard is the International Maritime Organization (IMO), a body of the United Nations, which sets international maritime vessel safety and marine pollution standards. The Coast Guard represents the United States at IMO meetings.

Multiple international conventions concern vessels and their impact on the marine environment. Described below are two selected conventions that contain provisions that are particularly relevant to oil pollution in coastal waters.

MARPOL 73/78

The IMO implements the 1973 International Convention for the Prevention of Pollution from Ships, as modified by the Protocol of 1978 (MARPOL 73/78).[109] Vessels whose nations are signatories to MARPOL are subject to its requirements, regardless of where they sail, and member nations are responsible for the vessels registered under their flag.

MARPOL 73/78 includes six annexes, each covering a different pollution type. Annex I (Prevention of Pollution by Oil) entered into force in 1983[110] and established requirements for controlling oil discharges to sea. Annex I requires vessels to have equipment that minimizes oil discharge, such as oil-water separators, and shipboard oil pollution emergency plans (SOPEPs). Although the SOPEP applicability is similar to that of the vessel response plan (VRP) required by OPA,[111] the purpose of the SOPEP is somewhat different. A SOPEP is intended to provide guidance to the vessel's officers regarding proper onboard emergency procedures when an oil spill occurs,[112] whereas the VRP is more focused on responding to the spill itself.

The United States implements Annex I through the Act to Prevent Pollution from Ships (APPS).[113] APPS applies to all U.S.-flagged ships, irrespective of location, and to all foreign-flagged vessels in U.S. waters or at ports under U.S. jurisdiction. The Coast Guard issues and enforces regulations necessary to carry out the APPS provisions. The USCG inspection program is a key component of its oil spill prevention effort.

---

[108] If a treaty is considered "self-executing," domestic legislation implementing the treaty is not necessary. For more details on these issues, see CRS Report RL32528, *International Law and Agreements: Their Effect Upon U.S. Law*, by Michael John Garcia.

[109] For convention texts and other materials, see http://www.imo.org.

[110] The phrase "entry into force" signifies that the requisite number of nations have ratified the convention or annex, thus making the agreed upon requirements binding for all participating nations. For more discussion of the procedures of international conventions, see the IMO website at http://www.imo.org.

[111] All vessels of any type over 400 gross tons traveling over international waters must have a SOPEP approved by their flag state. See USCG VRP/SOPEP "FAQs" at http://www.uscg.mil/vrp.

[112] USCG, 1997, *Marine Safety Manual, Marine Environment Protection, Volume IX*, p. 4-24.

[113] P.L. 96-478, 33 U.S.C. 1901 et seq.

Intervention Convention

The 1967 *Torrey Canyon* spill off the coast of Great Britain was one of the first major spills to receive worldwide attention.[114] The incident raised many questions regarding oil spill response, particularly when dealing with vessels from other nations. For example, the incident prompted debate over responses allowable if a nation's waters and environment are threatened by a spill from another nation's vessel. The 1969 International Convention Relating to Intervention on the High Seas in Cases of Oil Pollution Casualties (the Intervention Convention) sought to address these issues.

To implement this convention in the United States, Congress passed the Intervention on the High Seas Act of 1974.[115] Under this act, if the Coast Guard determines there to be a "grave and imminent danger to the coastline or related interests of the United States from pollution or threat of pollution of the sea by convention oil [i.e., as defined in the convention]," the Coast Guard can take action to "prevent, mitigate, or eliminate that danger."

State Laws

As mentioned above, multiple states had oil spill liability laws before the passage of OPA in 1990. During the 15 years prior to OPA's passage, the issue of whether or not to preempt state liability laws was perhaps the primary obstacle to enacting unified oil spill legislation. Proponents of preemption argued that differing state laws—particularly the various levels of liability—frustrate the shipping industry and were contrary to the goal of comprehensive federal legislation. Preemption opponents maintained that states should be allowed (as with most other federal environmental statutes) to set stiffer standards regarding liability, compensation, and cleanup.[116] In the aftermath of the *Exxon Valdez* spill, the scales tipped to the side of anti-preemption. According to OPA Section 1018 (referred to as a "savings clause"), the act will not preempt any state from imposing "additional liability or requirements" with respect to the discharge of oil or related response activity (e.g., cleanup standards). A 2003 study identified 16 states that impose unlimited liability for oil spills.[117]

There was some concern that the language of OPA's savings clause would allow states to regulate matters typically reserved for the federal government, such as oil tanker construction. To address this issue, the conference report stated that the savings clause would not disturb a 1978 Supreme Court decision that dealt with the intersection of federal and state authority to regulate the shipping industry.[118] In that case, the Court determined that a Washington State law was

---

[114] The *Torrey Canyon*, a Liberian-flagged tanker, spilled approximately 35 million gallons of crude oil.

[115] P.L. 93-248 , 33 U.S.C. 1471 et seq.

[116] One argument against preemption was that existing requirements under particular state laws would be diminished or negated entirely. See Benjamin Grumbles and Joan Manley, "The Oil Pollution Act of 1990: Legislation in the Wake of a Crisis," *Natural Resources and Environment*, 10:2 (1995), p. 38.

[117] Dagmar Etkin, 2003, *A Worldwide Review of Marine Oil Spill Fines and Penalties*, at http://www.environmental-research.com/erc_papers/ERC_paper_10.pdf. See also, CRS Congressional Distribution Memorandum, "Oil Spill Liability in the Gulf States," July 2, 2010 (on file with author).

[118] U.S. Congress, Conference Report accompanying H.R. 1465, Oil Pollution Act of 1990, H. Conf. Rept. 101-653, at 122 (1990).

preempted. The state law had attempted to govern oil tanker design, size, and movement in Puget Sound.[119]

Regardless of the clarification in the conference report, the line between federal and state jurisdiction (i.e., the extent of federal preemption) continues to be tested. In 2000, the Supreme Court struck down (as preempted) a Washington State rule calling for various personnel requirements, such as training, on oil tankers.[120] Similarly, in March 2010, a federal district court in Massachusetts ruled against a state law—finding it preempted—that would affect tanker design, personnel qualifications, and navigation.[121]

Conclusion

With the nation a significant producer and consumer of oil, vast quantities are continuously extracted, imported, and transported throughout the United States. Oil is expected to remain a primary source of energy in the United States for at least the next several decades. Future oil spills are inevitable.

As with the *Exxon Valdez* oil spill in 1989, the 2010 *Deepwater Horizon* spill has generated significant interest in various oil spill policy matters, including prevention, preparedness, response, and liability and compensation. Policymakers have begun to examine each of these components, and future scrutiny is expected, particularly as various analyses and recommendations from related investigations and commissions are completed and made public.

Author Contact Information

Jonathan L. Ramseur
Specialist in Environmental Policy
jramseur@crs.loc.gov, 7-7919

---

[119] *Ray v. Atlantic Richfield*, 435 U.S. 151 (1978).

[120] *United States v. Locke*, 529 U.S. 89 (2000).

[121] *United States v. Massachusetts*, 2010 Westlaw 1345018 (D. Mass. March 31, 2010).

CPSIA information can be obtained at www.ICGtesting.com
Printed in the USA
BVOW06s1127290713

327229BV00011B/316/P